A Cab Man

by Clint Campo
illustrated by Hector Borlasca

Practice Decodable 17

McGraw Hill Education

Bothell, WA • Chicago, IL • Columbus, OH • New York, NY

MHEonline.com

Send all inquiries to:
McGraw-Hill Education
8787 Orion Place
Columbus, OH 43240

ISBN: 978-0-02-132724-9
MHID: 0-02-132724-6

Printed in China

8 9 10 11 12 DSS 27 26 25 24 23

Scott is a cab man.

Scott has a cab cap.

And Scott has a cab!

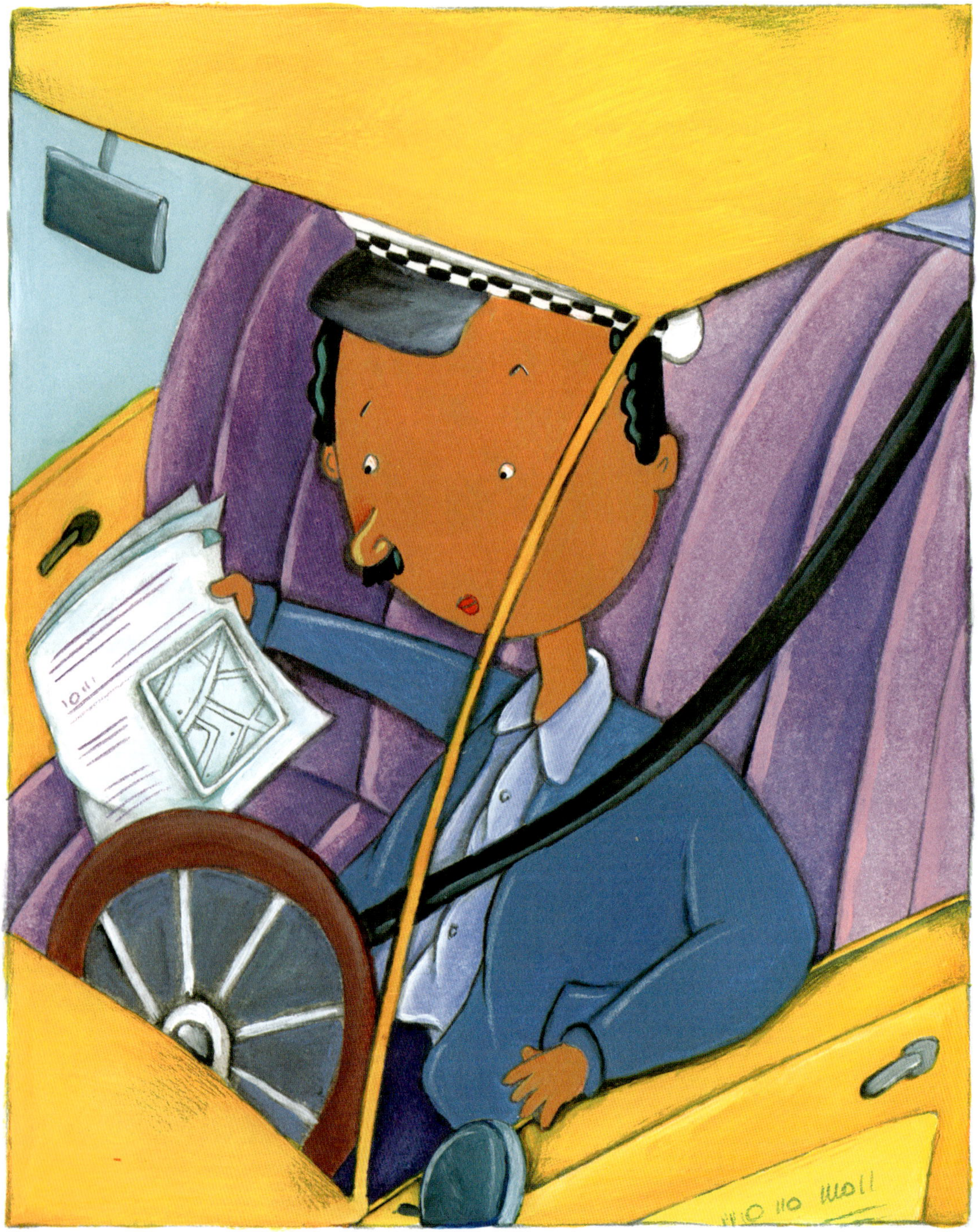

Scott can see a cab map.

Scott is a sad cab man.

Scott's cab sits and sits!